A+ books

Bilingual Picture Dictionaries

My First Book of
Korean
Words

apple
사과
(sa-gwa)

by Katy R. Kudela

Translator: Translations.com

CAPSTONE PRESS
a capstone imprint

Table of Contents

How to Use This Dictionary

This book is full of useful words in both Korean and English. The English word appears first, followed by the Korean word. Look below each Korean word for help to sound it out. Try reading the words aloud.

Topic Heading in English

Topic Heading in Korean

Word in English
Word in Korean
(pronunciation)

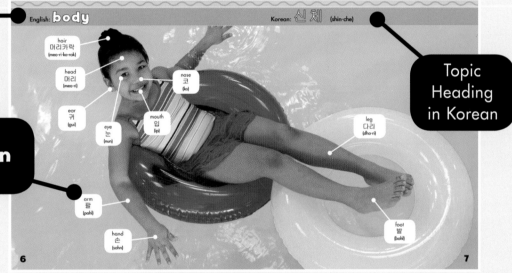

English: **body**   Korean: 신체 (shin-che)

hair
머리카락
(meo-ri-ka-rak)

head
머리
(meo-ri)

nose
코
(ko)

ear
귀
(gui)

eye
눈
(nun)

mouth
입
(ip)

leg
다리
(da-ri)

arm
팔
(pahl)

hand
손
(sohn)

foot
발
(bahl)

6   7

Notes about the Korean Language

The Korean alphabet is named Hangeul (or Hangul). This alphabet has 24 letters, including 14 consonants and 10 vowels.

In Korean, the letters are combined together into syllable blocks. Most pronunciations are evenly stressed. However, pronunciations with double letters give the letter sounds more emphasis.

Unlike English, double vowels are not separated into two syllables.

To read the Korean characters, look at the pronunciation. The pronunciations can be read like English.

Depending on the meaning, some English words are represented by more than one Korean word. Commas are used to separate the words in these labels.

uncle
삼촌, 이모부, 고모부
(sam-chon, e-mo-bu, go-mo-bu)

mother
어머니
(eo-meo-ni)

cousin
사촌
(sa-chon)

aunt
이모, 고모, 숙모
(ee-mo, go-mo, suk-mo)

baby
아기
(ah-ghee)

4

grandmother
할머니
(hal-meo-ni)

father
아버지
(a-beo-ji)

grandfather
할아버지
(hal-a-beo-ji)

brother
형, 남동생
(hyeong, nam-dong-saeng)

sister
언니, 여동생
(eon-ni, yeo-dong-saeng)

hair
머리카락
(meo-ri-ka-rak)

head
머리
(meo-ri)

nose
코
(ko)

ear
귀
(gui)

mouth
입
(ip)

eye
눈
(nun)

arm
팔
(pahl)

hand
손
(sohn)

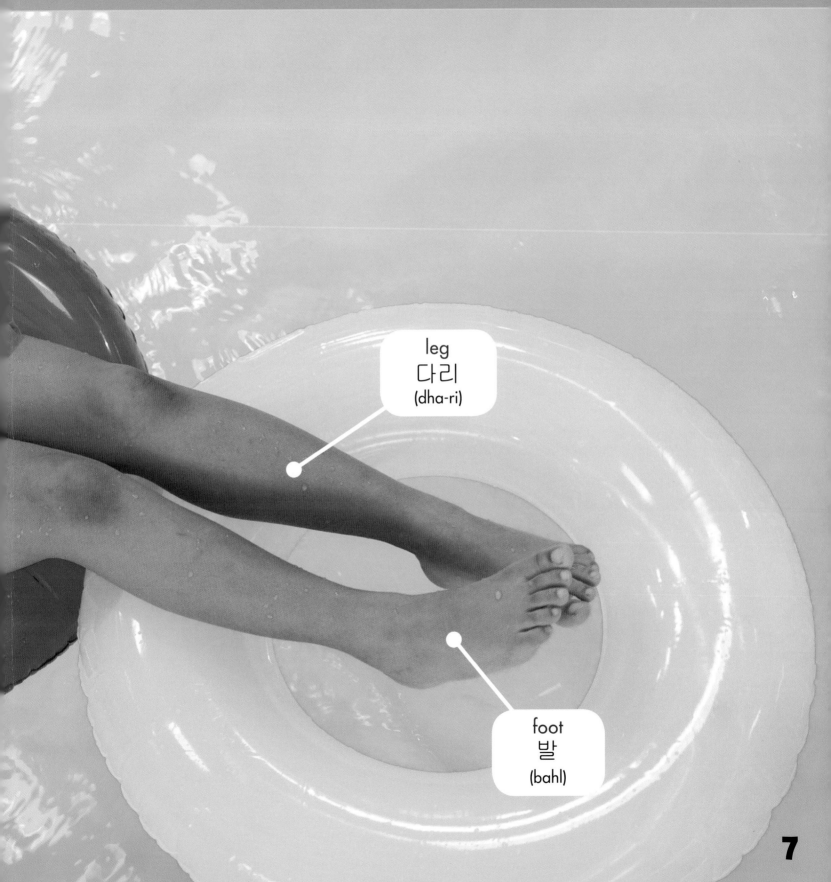

leg
다리
(dha-ri)

foot
발
(bahl)

pajamas
파자마
(pa-ja-ma)

coat
코트
(ko-teu)

shorts
반바지
(bhan-bah-ji)

boot
부츠
(bu-tseu)

8

shoe
신발
(shin-bahl)

hat
모자
(mo-ja)

pants
바지
(bah-ji)

sock
양말
(yang-mahl)

dress
드레스
(d-re-sseu)

shirt
셔츠
(sheo-steu)

9

kite
연
(yeon)

doll
인형
(in-hyeong)

puzzle
퍼즐
(peo-zle)

train
기차
(ghi-cha)

wagon
4륜차
(sa-ryun-cha)

puppet
꼭두각시
(kkok-du-ghak-shi)

skateboard
스케이트보드
(s-ke-i-teu-bo-deu)

jump rope
줄넘기
(jul-neom-ghi)

ball
공
(gong)

bat
배트
(bae-teu)

picture
사진
(sa-jin)

lamp
램프
(lam-peu)

window
창문
(chang-mun)

dresser
화장대
(hwa-jang-dae)

curtain
커튼
(keo-teun)

blanket
담요
(dahm-yo)

12

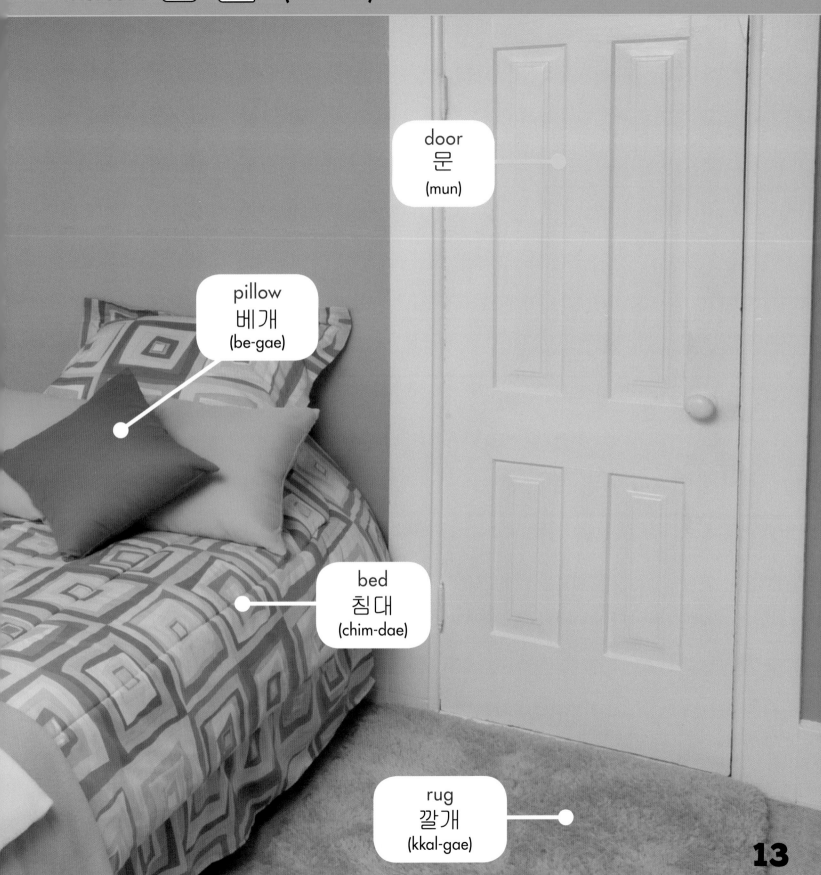

door
문
(mun)

pillow
베개
(be-gae)

bed
침대
(chim-dae)

rug
깔개
(kkal-gae)

bathtub
욕조
(yok-jo)

soap
비누
(bi-nu)

toilet
변기
(byeon-ghi)

14

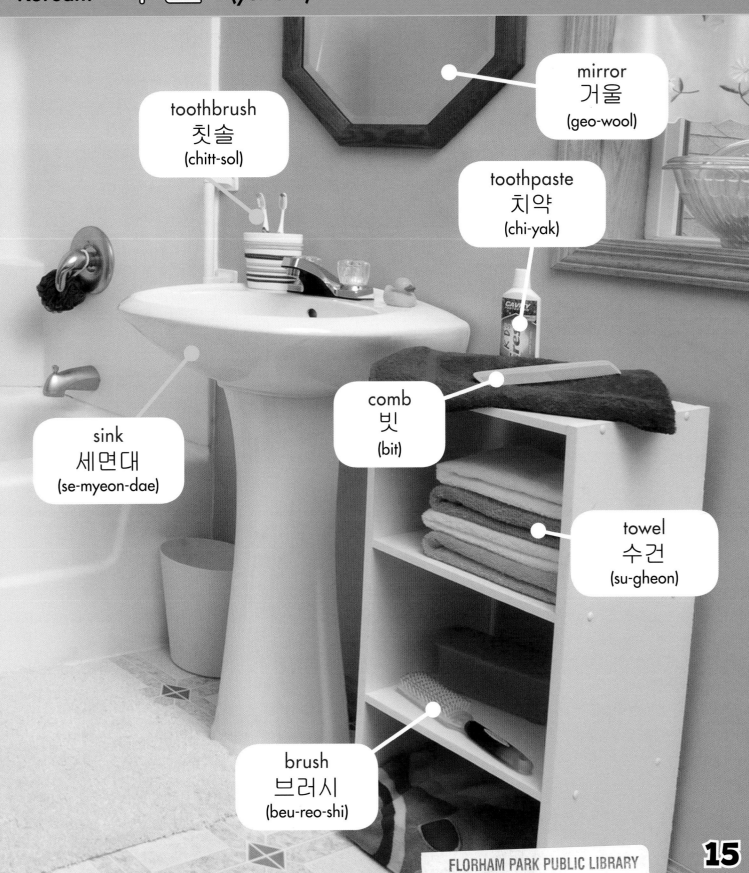

mirror
거울
(geo-wool)

toothbrush
칫솔
(chitt-sol)

toothpaste
치약
(chi-yak)

comb
빗
(bit)

sink
세면대
(se-myeon-dae)

towel
수건
(su-gheon)

brush
브러시
(beu-reo-shi)

pot
냄비
(naem-bi)

stove
가스 레인지
(ga-s re-in-gi)

bowl
사발
(sah-bahl)

oven
오븐
(o-beun)

16

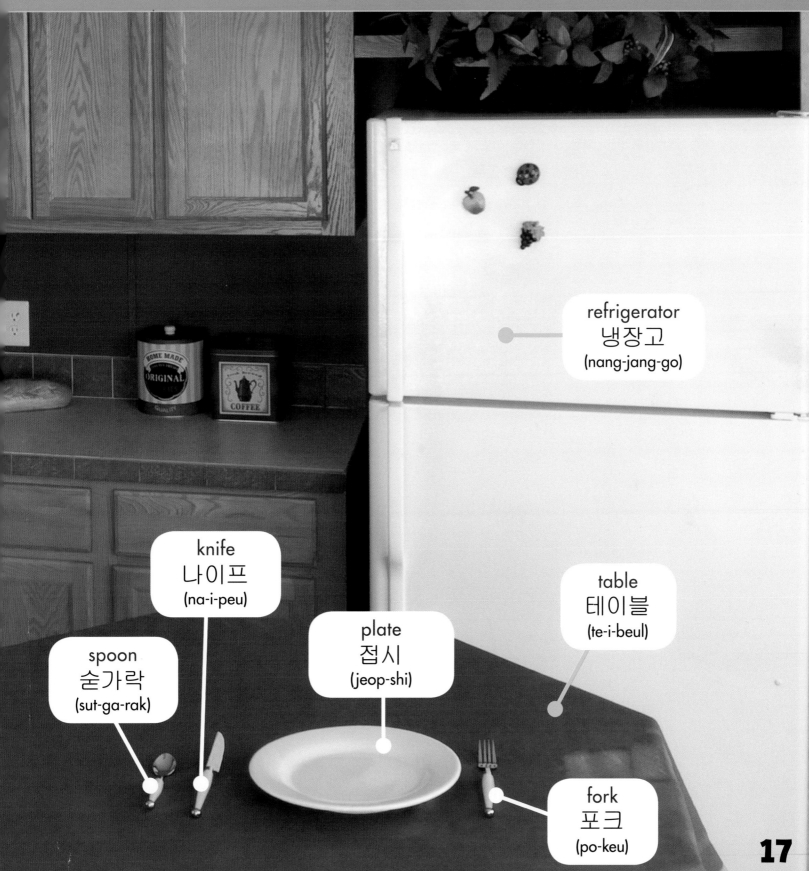

refrigerator
냉장고
(nang-jang-go)

knife
나이프
(na-i-peu)

table
테이블
(te-i-beul)

plate
접시
(jeop-shi)

spoon
숟가락
(sut-ga-rak)

fork
포크
(po-keu)

17

milk
우유
(woo-yu)

carrot
당근
(dang-geun)

bread
브레드
(b-re-d)

apple
사과
(sa-gwa)

butter
버터
(beo-teo)

Salted Sweet Cream
Butter
NET WT 4 OZ (1/4 LB) 113.4 g

Salted Sweet Cream
Butter
NET WT 4 OZ (1/4 LB) 113.4 g

egg
계란
(gye-ran)

pea
완두콩
(wan-du-kong)

orange
오렌지
(o-ren-ji)

sandwich
샌드위치
(san-d-wi-chi)

rice
쌀, 밥
(ssal, bab)

tractor
트랙터
(teu-rac-teo)

hay
건초
(geon-cho)

fence
울타리
(ul-ta-ri)

farmer
농부
(nong-bu)

sheep
양
(yang)

pig
돼지
(doai-ji)

horse
말
(mahl)

barn
헛간
(hut-gahn)

cow
젖소
(jeot-so)

chicken
닭
(dahk)

21

leaf
잎
(ip)

butterfly
나비
(na-bi)

flower
꽃
(kkot)

shovel
삽
(sap)

bird
새
(sae)

worm
벌레
(beol-le)

plant
식물
(sik-mul)

grass
잔디
(jan-di)

dirt
흙
(heuk)

seed
씨앗
(ssi-at)

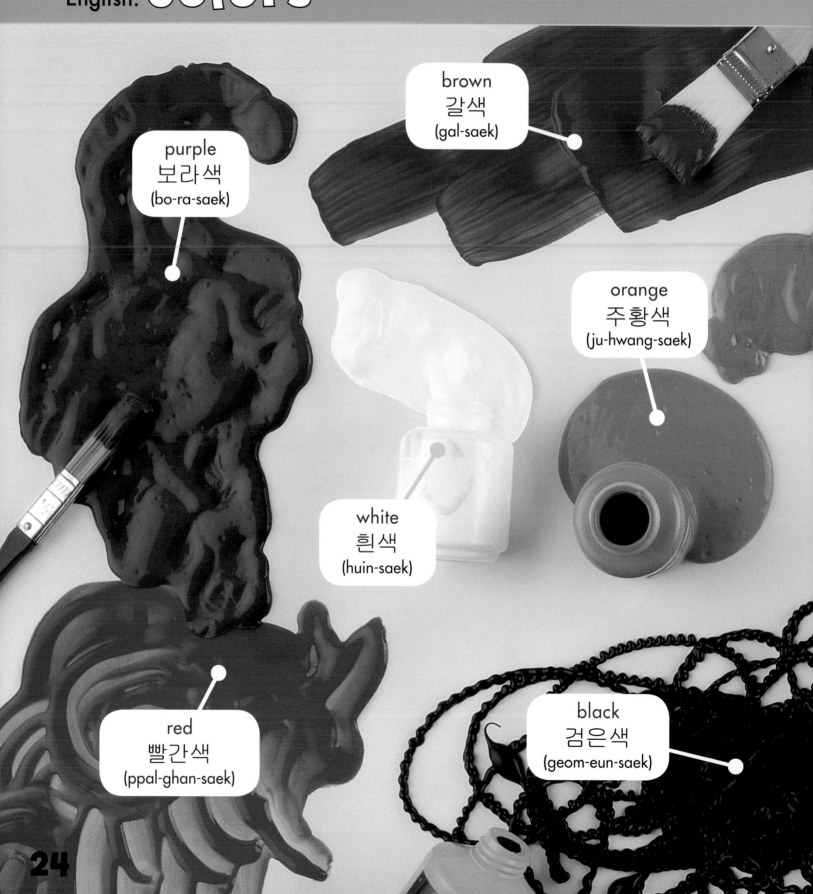

brown
갈색
(gal-saek)

purple
보라색
(bo-ra-saek)

orange
주황색
(ju-hwang-saek)

white
흰색
(huin-saek)

red
빨간색
(ppal-ghan-saek)

black
검은색
(geom-eun-saek)

pink
분홍색
(bun-hong-saek)

blue
파란색
(pa-ran-saek)

yellow
노란색
(no-ran-saek)

green
초록색
(cho-rok-saek)

teacher
선생님
(seon-saeng-nim)

book
책
(chaek)

desk
책상
(chaek-sahng)

pencil
연필
(yeon-pil)

crayon
크레용
(k-re-yong)

26

map
지도
(ji-do)

clock
시계
(shi-gye)

computer
컴퓨터
(keom-pyu-teo)

chair
의자
(ui-ja)

paper
종이
(jong-e)

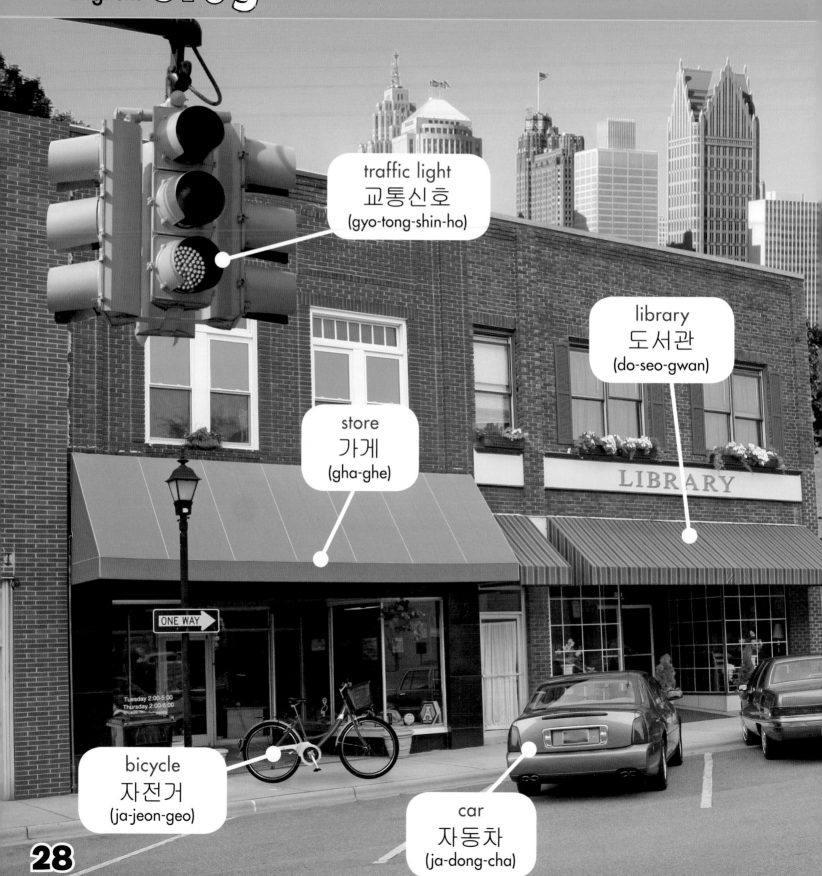

traffic light
교통신호
(gyo-tong-shin-ho)

library
도서관
(do-seo-gwan)

store
가게
(gha-ghe)

bicycle
자전거
(ja-jeon-geo)

car
자동차
(ja-dong-cha)

LIBRARY

ONE WAY

Tuesday 2:00-5:00
Thursday 2:00-6:00

tree
나무
(na-mu)

bus
버스
(beo-seu)

park
공원
(gong-won)

street
거리
(geo-ri)

sign
간판
(ghan-pahn)

Numbers • 숫자 (sutt-ja)

1. one • 일 (il)
2. two • 이 (e)
3. three • 삼 (sahm)
4. four • 사 (sah)
5. five • 오 (o)

6. six • 육 (yuk)
7. seven • 칠 (chil)
8. eight • 팔 (pahl)
9. nine • 구 (gu)
10. ten • 십 (sip)

Useful Phrases • 유용한 구문 (yu-yong-han gu-mun)

yes • 예 (ye)

no • 아니오 (ah-ni-o)

hello • 안녕하세요 (ahn-nyeong-ha-se-yo)

good-bye • 안녕히 가세요 (ahn-nyeong-hi ghah-se-yo)

good morning • 좋은 아침입니다 (jo-eun ah-chim-im-ni-dah)

good night • 안녕히 주무세요 (ahn-nyeong-hi ju-mu-se-yo)

please • 제발 (je-bahl)

thank you • 감사합니다 (gahm-sah-ham-ni-dah)

excuse me • 실례합니다 (shil-lye-ham-ni-dah)

My name is _____. • 제 이름은_____ 입니다. (je i-reum-eun _____ im-ni-dah)

Read More

Mahoney, Judy. *Teach Me Everyday Korean.* Minnetonka, Minn.: Teach Me Tapes, 2008.

Turhan, Sedat. *Milet Mini Picture Dictionary: English-Korean.* London: Milet Publishing, 2005.

Internet Sites

FactHound offers a safe, fun way to find Internet sites related to this book. All of the sites on FactHound have been researched by our staff.

Here's all you do:

Visit *www.facthound.com*

Type in this code: 9781429659635

Super-cool stuff!

Check out projects, games and lots more at
www.capstonekids.com

A+ Books an
1710 Roe Crest Driv
www.capstonepub.com

Library of Congress Cataloging-in-Publication Data
Kudela, Katy R.
    My first book of Korean words / by Katy R. Kudela.
    p. cm. — (A+ Books, Bilingual picture dictionaries)
    Includes bibliographical references.
    Summary: "Simple text paired with themed photos invite the reader to learn to speak Korean"—
Provided by publisher.
    ISBN 978-1-4296-5963-5 (library binding)
    ISBN 978-1-4296-6165-2 (paperback)
    1. Picture dictionaries, Korean. 2. Picture dictionaries, English. 3. Korean language—Dictionaries,
Juvenile—English. 4. English language—Dictionaries, Juvenile—Korean. I. Title. II. Series.
PL939.K83 2010
495.7'321–dc22   2010029471

Credits
Lori Bye, designer; Wanda Winch, media researcher; Eric Manske, production specialist

Photo Credits
Capstone Studio/Gary Sundermeyer, cover (pig), 20 (farmer with tractor, pig)
Capstone Studio/Karon Dubke, cover (ball, sock), 1, 3, 4–5, 6–7, 8–9, 10–11, 12–13,
    14–15, 16–17, 18–19, 22–23, 24–25, 26–27
Image Farm, back cover, 1, 2, 31, 32 (design elements)
iStockphoto/Andrew Gentry, 28 (main street)
Photodisc, cover (flower)
Shutterstock/Adrian Matthiassen, cover (butterfly); David Hughes, 20 (hay); Eric Isselee,
    20–21 (horse); hamurishi, 28 (bike); Ievgeniia Tikhonova, 21 (chickens); Jim Mills, 29
    (stop sign); Kelli Westfal, 28 (traffic light); Margo Harrison, 20 (sheep); MaxPhoto, 21
    (cow and calf); Melinda Fawver, 29 (bus); Robert Elias, 20–21 (barn, fence); Vladimir
    Mucibabic, 28–29 (city skyline)

Note to Parents, Teachers, and Librarians
Learning to speak a second language at a young age has been shown to improve overall
academic performance, boost problem-solving ability, and foster an appreciation for other
cultures. Early exposure to language skills provides a strong foundation for other subject
areas, including math and reasoning. Introducing children to a second language can help
to lay the groundwork for future academic success and cultural awareness.

Printed in China by Nordica.
0913/CA21301845
082013   007688R